YOUR KNOWLEDGE HAS VALUE

An Introduction to RISC V. "Reduced Instruction Set Computer" Processor

Arpita Patel

Bibliographic information published by the German National Library:

The German National Library lists this publication in the National Bibliography; detailed bibliographic data are available on the Internet at http://dnb.dnb.de.

ISBN: 9783389028421
This book is also available as an ebook.

Print and binding: Books on Demand GmbH, Norderstedt, Germany
Printed on acid-free paper from responsible sources.

The present work has been carefully prepared. Nevertheless, authors and publishers do not incur liability for the correctness of information, notes, links and advice as well as any printing errors.

GRIN web shop: https://www.grin.com/document/1477029

An introduction to RISC V - "Reduced Instruction set Computer" Processor

RISC-V, an open-source Instruction Set Architecture (ISA), has become a significant performer in the realm of computer architecture, challenging traditional proprietary designs and opening the doors for innovation and customization. Initially in this work, RISC-V's historical evolution, its architecture, including its design concepts, instruction set, register file and implementations, were understood through a literature survey. A comprehensive literature survey is conducted on various variants of RISC-V family and their applications, which include lowering total costs, speeding up processor execution, consuming less power, and creating a more manageable and compact versions of the original architecture. The study includes a thorough analysis of several RISC-V variations. According to review of the literature, the 32-bit biRISC-V processor core is the newest member of the RISC-V family and using superscalar dual issue design to increase processor overall throughput.

I

CONTENTS

ABSTRACT I

CONTENTS.. II

LIST OF FIGURES IV

LIST OF TABLES IV

1 Introduction to RISC-V 1

1.1 Background… 1

1.2 History of RISC-V 2

1.3 Objective of the work..3

1.4 RISC-V Architecure..4

1.5 RISC-V overview..4

1.6 RISC VS CISC Processor 5

    1.6.1 RISC Processor 5

    1.6.2 CISC Processor 6

1.7 RISC-V Features...7

1.8 RISC-V Processor Extensions 7

    1.8.1 RISC-V Bases 8

    1.8.2 RISC-V Extensions 8

1.9 RISC-V Instruction set..9

1.10 RISC-V Registers...10

1.11 Major Contribution 11

1.12 Summary..12

2 Literature Survey on RISC-V...13

2.1 Single Cycle RISC-V Micro Architecture Processor and its FPGA Prototype.......................13

2.2 Reconfigurable RISC-V Secure Processor and SoC Integration 15

2.3 Single Cycle 64-Bit RISCV Processor and it's FPGA Prototype...16

2.4 Design of Adjacent Interconnect Processor Based on RISC-V..17

2.5 Design and Implementation of a RISC V Processor on FPGA...18

2.6 Implementation of the RISC-V Architecture with the Extended Zbb Instruction Set 20

2.7 A RISC-V ISA Compatible Processor IP 21

2.8 Implementation and Extension of Bit Manipulation Instruction on RISC-V Architecture

using FPGA...22

2.9 biRISC-V... 23

3 Comclusion..26
References..26

III

LIST OF FIGURES

1.1 : RISC-V Instruction Set.. 10

2.1 : Top Level Logical Overview… 14

2.2 : Adjacency interconnection mechanism simulation waveform 19

2.3 : Dhyrstone Benchmark Performance 20

LIST OF TABLES

1.1 Difference between of RISC vs CISC.. 6

1.2 RISC-V Registers..11

2.1 Design Utilization Summary...15

2.2 Hardware Utilization and Peak Operating Frequency 16

2.3 Design summary of Developed System 17

2.4 Adjacent Interconnection Instructions 18

2.5 FPGA Utilization Metrics 20

2.6 Comparison of Processor Cores with Basic and Extended Architecture 21

2.7 Prediction accuracy improvement..22

2.8 Performance improvement in synthetic benchmarks 22

2.9 Resource Utilization...23

2.10 Comprehensive Analysis 24

Chapter 1 Introduction to RISC-V

1.1 Background

The definition, description, and specifications of a computer processor core's operation are provided by an Instruction Set Architecture (ISA) specific to that specific computer. At the machine level, each instruction and register are described by ISA. ISA explains the functions of each instruction and how it is coded into bit.

The interface between software and hardware is called ISA [1]. Digital circuits are designed by hardware developers according to the particular ISA definition. Code is written by software developers in compliance with a particular ISA definition. ISA refers to the set of instructions that a computer processor can understand and execute [1].

These existing ISA standards are all quite complicated and proprietary. Certain ISA specifics are not made public at all, although you can find the details in comprehensive manuals. Furthermore, ISA have a limited design, such as backward compatibility, and have been in a use for a long time. Older work can provide us with further computer-aided design ideas. Today's best design choices have also been impacted by advancements in silicon hardware technology.

Because it specifies a processor's capabilities and functions, ISA is essential to computing. It gives programmers a standardized method for creating applications that work with many computer architectures. Software can be written once and run on multiple hardware systems by following an ISA, which improves portability and compatibility [1].

1

Researchers from the University of California, Berkeley created an open Instruction Set Architecture (ISA) based on Reduced Instruction Set Computers (RISC) principles in response to the growing amount of instructions in popular Instruction Set Architectures (ISA) and the demands of earlier extensions [1]. The purpose of this architecture, known as RISC-V [1], is to help software engineers with a minimal and robust ISA by offering both base ISA and application-specific extensions.

Complex Instruction Set Computing (CISC) was the most popular architecture in the early days of computing. Numerous complex machine language instructions that can carry out several tasks in a single instruction define CISC architecture. When memory was a major cost component, this strategy was initially advantageous because it made memory use more efficient.

ISAs required license fees, provided restricted access to internal information and architecture, and were entirely regulated by specific company types. This kind of limitation reduced innovation and makes it harder for start-up businesses to develop and produce new processors. Thus, RISC-V was used as a result. Numerous RISC processors, including PowerPC and SPARC, existed prior to RISC-V. Although this design had license costs and had limited working capabilities, it was still deemed useful and employed in several applications.

1.2 History of RISC-V

RISC-V was developed at the University of California. It was first created as a research projectin 2010. This project aimed to create new open-source ISAs with the capability to handle the limitations of previous ISAs and provide functionality to create new processors. Computer experts Andrew Waterman, Yunsup Lee, and Krste Asanović led this initiative, drawing inspiration from the success of open-source software to create new hardware benefits.

Based on the instruction set, the first iteration of the RISC-V ISA, known as RV31, was published in 2011. Its original introduction follows the principles of RISC and is based on simplicity and efficiency. As time went on, RISC-V ISA added new features and extensions to expand its capabilities and address large-area applications. In order to utilize and promote the RISC-V ISA, the RISC-V Foundation was established in 2015. Collaboration between businesses, academic institutions, and individual students interested in participating in the advancement of RISC-V technology created this foundation.

1.3 Objective of the work

The purpose of this report is to explain the RISC-V ISA. It will focus on the design concepts, special features, and historical evolution of RISC-V. It will also function as an educational tool, offering a comprehensive grasp of the architecture. The effects it has had on the computing landscape and semiconductor business. Students, engineers, academics, and beginners can all benefit from learning about RISC-V as an alternative instruction set architecture and its possible uses. This paper contributes to the understanding of the technical elements of RISC-V by contrasting its performance, power efficiency, scalability, and versatility with those of other architectures, such as ARM or x86.

When started learning about the RISC-V architecture by doing the literature survey about how the RISC-V architecture is developed over the years till today, there are so many different

3

architectures have been developed based on this RISC-V architecture principles by keeping in mind to different possibilities like to reduced the cost of the developed architecture, to reduced power consumption of developed architecture, to increase the performance of the developed architecture, to minimize the time to complete the process, use of less clock cycle to complete the process. So during the learning process came across this biRISC-V processor which discuss the fundamental of increase the throughput of the processor by using superscalar architecture with dual issuing instruction concept.

1.4 RISC-V Architecture

The instruction set architecture (ISA) known as RISC-V was first created to help in computer architecture research and instruction. The base integer ISA, which is a must for every implementation, and optional additions to the base ISA are what provide up the RISC-V ISA. Traditional proprietary ISAs include a number of essential principles and features that form the foundation of the RISC-V instruction set architectural design. The RISC-V specification is a set of ISA alternatives rather than a single ISA.

Because of the architecture's ability to give the processor more straightforward instructions to complete a variety of jobs, RISC-V has grown in popularity. It also speeds up time to market by allowing designers to generate thousands of possible customized processors.

1.5 RISC-V Architecture overview

The base integer ISA is remarkably similar to the early RISC CPU, With the exception of the lack of branch delay slots and support for optional variable-length instruction encodings. In order to enable convenient ISA, the base is deliberately limited to the bare minimum set of instructions needed to serve as a viable target for operating systems, assemblers, linkers, and compilers [2].

The width of the integer and the matching size of the user address space define each base integer instruction set. RV32I and RV64I are the two main base integer variations that offer 32-bit or 64-bit user level address spaces, respectively. To support small microcontrollers, the RV32E subset variation of the RV32I base instruction set has been added [2].

RISC design executes a single instruction every clock cycle, compared to complex instruction set computing (CISC), which uses a bigger set of more complicated instructions for multiple procedures per instruction. Even complex operations can be completed with a small amount of instruction. Because of this, designs are simplified and use less energy, and decoding can be finished quickly.

1.6 RISC VS CISC Processor

1.6.1 RISC Processor

Reduced Instruction Set Computer Processors, or RISC microprocessors, are microprocessor architectures that have a highly specialized set of instructions that are simple to compile. It is designed to optimize and restrict the number of instructions in order to reduce the execution time of an instruction. It indicates that there is just one clock cycle needed for each instruction cycle, which has three parameters: fetch, decode, and execute. By dividing complex instructions into simpler ones, the RISC processor can also carry out a variety of complex tasks. Because RISC devices use several transistors, they are less expensive to develop and require less time to execute instructions.

1.6.2 CISC Processor

The Complex Instruction Set Computer, or CISC, is the short form for the device. It has a wide variety of complex instructions that different in complexity from basic to highly specialized at the assembly language level, resulting in a lengthy execution time. In order to reduce the amount of instructions on each program and ignore the number of cycles per instruction, CISC takes this strategy. The idea is to include complex instructions directly into the hardware, as hardware is generally faster than software. CISC chips consume less instructions than RISC chips, however they are still comparatively slower than RISC CPUs.

Table 1.1 : Difference between RISC vs CISC

RISC	CISC
It stands for Reduced Instruction Set Computer.	It stands for Complex Instruction Set Computer.
Simple instructions are executed in one clock cycle.	Architecture has a set of special purpose circuits which help execute the instructions at a high speed.
These chips are relatively simple to design.	These chips are complex to design.
It has less number of instructions.	It has more number of instructions.
It has fixed-length encodings for instructions.	It has variable-length encodings of instructions.

1.7 RISC-V Features

Openness : RISC-V's open source architecture is one of its main advantages. Because the ISA is publicly available, developers can create, produce, and market RISC-V-based processors without worrying about royalties or licensing costs. The fact that RISC-V development is open to the academic community, business community, and individual developers to inspires cooperation, knowledge exchange, and broad innovation.

Modularity : To satisfy particular needs, new instruction set extensions, including those for vector processing, cryptography, floating-point operations, and more, can be implemented. Because of its modularity, developers can customize RISC-V processors to meet specific demands and cut down on the complexity and expense of extraneous features.

Simplicity : RISC-V enhances verification procedures and improves implementation by reducing complexity. This focus on simplicity improves RISC-V processor speed, security, and dependability. Additionally, it allows quick development, prototyping, and debugging, which speeds up the innovation cycle.

1.8 RISC-V Processor Extensions

RISC-V is built for high levels of specialization and customization. One or more optional instruction set extensions may be added to the base integer ISA, but the base integer instruction itself cannot be modified. Thus, there are two categories of RISC-V instruction set extensions: standard and non-standard [3][4].

Comparing Standard and Non-Standard Extension A basic integer ISA (RV32I or RV64I) must be supported by any implementation of a RISC-V processor. Other than that, one or more extensions may be supported by an implementation. Extensions fall into one of two main categories: standard or non-standard [3][4].

Standard Extensions : Predefined sets of instructions known as standard extensions are created to target specific applications or satisfy certain needs. Several standard extensions are defined by the RISC-V specification and are identified by single-letter abbreviations. The base integer instruction set for 32-bit or 64-bit implementations, for instance, is RV32I/RV64I.

Custom Extensions : The modularity of RISC-V enables the development of unique extensions specific to particular applications. Specifically, the standard RISC-V specification does not include custom extensions. Custom extensions might provide improved performance or capabilities for particular workloads by enabling domain-specific optimizations, accelerators, or specialized operations.

1.8.1 RISC-V Bases

- RV32I – Base Integer Instruction Set, 32-bit
- RV64I – Base Integer Instruction Set, 64-bit
- RV128I – Base Integer Instruction Set, 128-bit
- RV32E – Base Integer Instruction Set (embedded), 32-bit, 16 registers with a smaller instruction set
- RV64E – Base Integer Instruction Set (embedded), 64-bit

8

1.8.2 RISC-V Extensions

- M – Standard Extension for Integer Multiplication and Division

- A – Standard Extension for Atomic Instructions

- F – Standard Extension for Single-Precision Floating-Point

- D – Standard Extension for Double-Precision Floating-Point

- B – Standard Extensions for Bit Manipulation

- T – Standard Extension for Transactional Memory

- V – Standard Extension for Vector Operations

1.9 RISC-V Instruction set

The RISC-V base is small. It contains just 47 instructions that everyone has to implement. It uses the simplest load/store architecture, which means that all operations are performed on the internal registers, and there are dedicated instructions to transfer between registers and memory. With only 47 instructions, the RV32I base integer ISA implements the absolutely necessary operations to achieve basic functionality with 32-bit integers (its 64-bit variant is RV64I). This ISA, encoded in 32-bits, includes instructions for:

- Addition

- Subtraction

- Bitwise operations

- Load and store

- Jumps

- Branches

31	30	25	24	21	20	19	15	14	12	11	8	7	6	0	
funct7			rs2			rs1		funct3		rd			opcode		R-type
imm[11:0]						rs1		funct3		rd			opcode		I-type
imm[11:5]			rs2			rs1		funct3		imm[4:0]			opcode		S-type
imm[12]	imm[10:5]		rs2			rs1		funct3		imm[4:1]	imm[11]		opcode		B-type
imm[31:12]										rd			opcode		U-type
imm[20]	imm[10:1]			imm[11]		imm[19:12]				rd			opcode		J-type

Figure 1.1 : RISC-V Instruction Set [6][11]

1.10 RISC-V Registers

The base ISA also specifies the 32 CPU registers, which are all 32-bits wide, plus the program counter. The only special register is x0, which always reads 0, as implemented in many previous RISC ISAs.

Although all registers are available for general purposes, the application binary interface specifies a purpose for each of them, according to its calling convention. This means that some registers are supposed to hold temporary or saved data, pointers, return addresses, and so on.

In addition to the argument and return value registers, five integer registers t0–t4 and six floating-point registers ft0–ft5 are temporary registers that are volatile across calls and must be saved by the caller if later used. Twelve integer registers s0–s11 and sixteen floating-point registers fs0–fs15 are preserved across calls and must be saved by the caller if used [5].

Table 1.2 : RISC-V Registers [4]

Register	ABI Name	Description	Saver
x0	zero	Hard-wired zero	-
x1	ra	Return address	Caller
x2	sp	Stack pointer	Caller
x3	gp	Global pointer	-
x4	tp	Thread pointer	-
x5	t0	Temporary/alternate link register	Caller
x6-7	t1-2	Temporaries	Caller
x8	s0/fp	Saved register/frame pointer	Caller
x9	s1	Saved register	Caller
x10-11	a0-1	Function arguments/return values	Caller
x12-17	a2-7	Function arguments	Caller
x18-27	s2-11	Saved registers	Caller
x28-31	t3-6	Temporaries	Caller
f0-7	ft0-7	FP temporaries	Caller
f8-9	fs0-1	FP saved registers	Caller
f10-11	fa0-1	FP arguments/return values	Caller
f12-17	fa2-7	FP arguments	Caller
f18-27	fs2-11	FP saved registers	Caller
f28-31	ft8-11	FP temporaries	Caller

1.11 Major Contribution

The procedures that have been carried out are detailed below:

1. I proceeded by studying RISC-V architecture its features, its extensions, its instruction set, its registers and other detail about RISC-V processor architecture.

2. A survey of the literature was conducted to learn more about the RISC-V ISA and the developments that have been made over time. This survey led to the discovery of the biRISC-V processor, which employs dual issue and superscalar designs. Several modules, including fetch, decode, execute, program counter, ALU, and issue, are contained in this biRISC-V processor.

11

3. Using the modelsim and quartus ii tools to simulate the biRISC-V module in Verilog and create test benches for each module to verify its operation.

1.12 Summary

With its modular, extensible, and open architecture, the RISC-V ISA is different from more conventional proprietary ISAs. The significance of RISC-V, its design ideas, and its historical development. The architecture and its capacity for transformation. The history of RISC-V shows the strength of open and collaborative innovation and highlights the relevance of this technology as a revolutionary force in the computer industry. This article aims to provide an overview of RISC-V, an open-source instruction set that inspires innovation and change in the computer industry. It also explains the history and implications of RISC-V. The RISC-V architecture, which offers an adaptable, modular, and extendable open-source ISA that can be customized to specific applications and use cases, marks a dramatic change in the field of processor design. Through the use of fundamental design concepts like modularity, extensibility, and reduced instruction set computing, RISC-V makes it possible to create processors with optimal power, performance, and affordability.

Chapter 2 Literature Survey on RISC-V

The instruction set architecture (ISA) also known as RISC-V (Reduced Instruction Set Computer - V) has drawn a lot of interest from both the semiconductor industry and the study of computer architecture. This review of the literature gives a summary of the most important educational and commercial works, highlighting the developments in technology, the historical background, and the effects of RISC-V on the computer environment.

2.1 Single Cycle RISC-V Micro Architecture Processor and its FPGA Prototype

The open-source RISC-V (RV32I) ISA is the foundation for the development of a fully synthesizable 32-bit CPU, which is shown. The intended market for this processor is low-cost embedded devices. This research also presents a framework for RISC-V development and validation that includes automated test suites and tool assembly. The end product is a low hardware complexity, one core, in-order, RISC-V processor that is not bus based [6].

This image has been removed due to copyright issues.

Figure 2.1 : Top Level Logical Overview [6]

The processor is further prototyped on an FPGA "Spartan 3E XC3S500E" board after being implemented in Verilog HDL. It has been determined that 32 MHz is the maximum operational frequency. Using the Xilinx Power Analyzer, the power is calculated to be 7.9 mW [6].

The authors have shared their work toward putting to work an entirely novel, highly flexible, single-cycle embedded processor design. 16KB of data memory and 64KB of instruction memory are used in on-chip block RAMs [6].

Table 2.1 : Design Utilization Summary [6]

Logic Utilization	Used
Total LUTs	5578
Number of FFs	1073
Number of slices	3393
RAM	1(512 x 32-bit)
ROM	1(64 x 32-bit)
Adder/Subtractor	313
Counters	1
Registers	1071
Comparators	312
Multiplexers	131
Logic shifters	3
XOR gates	4

2.2 Reconfigurable RISC-V Secure Processor and SoC Integration

Concerns about security in Internet of Things applications are gaining more and more attention. Nevertheless, cryptographic protection mechanisms are absent from embedded computers today [7].

Because of RISC-V openness and flexibility, an austere RISC-V core processor with RV32I subset instruction has been identified as a master device to work with an AES cryptography engine in a SoC [7].

This core includes a combination of independent instructions and a data bus that is linked to a Wishbone crossbar. The architecture protocol verification platform used is a Spartan-6 XC6SLX9 board, whose encryption SoC operates at 111.5 MHz and the RISC-V core at 105 MHz, respectively. When comparing the hardware resource use to the MIPS core with the same amount of effort, it is lower [7].

Table 2.2 : Hardware Utilization and Peak Operating Frequency [7]

Core	Slice	LUT	DFF	RAM	Peak Freq
MIPS32I[4]	574	1998	1749	48	107.479 MHz
RV32I	498	1796	1844	48	105.108 MHz

2.3 Single Cycle 64-Bit RISCV Processor and it's FPGA Prototype

The open-source RISC-V (RV64I) ISA is the base for the development of a fully synthesizable 64-bit CPU, which is shown. The purpose of this CPU is to provide to low-cost embedded devices. The end product is a low hardware complexity, one core, in-order, RISC-V processor that is not bus based [8].

Table 2.3 : Design summary of Developed System [8]

Device Utilization Summary(estimated values)			
Logic utilization	**Used**	**Available**	**Utilization**
Number of size registers	2015	93120	2%
Number of slice LUTs	4707	46560	10%
Number of fully used LUT-FF pairs	2013	4709	42%
Number of bonded IOBs	232	240	96%
Number of BUFG/BUFGCTRLs	1	32	3%

The suggested CPU is further prototyped on an FPGA "Spartan 6" board and implemented in Verilog HDL. The maximum operational frequency of 140.398 MHz has been determined. The Xilinx Power Analyzer estimates the power to be 0.037 W [8].

2.4 Design of Adjacent Interconnect Processor Based on RISC-V

The processor design of a reconfigurable array with adjacency interconnect, which is based on RISC-V architecture, is implemented by adding circuits and instructions for adjacency interconnect and implementing the standard five-stage pipeline structure [9].

Table 2.4 : Adjacent Interconnection Instructions [9]

Num	Assembly	Describe	Note
1	CORR NUM	Inter R ← IO	The processor writes the adjacency interconnect interface data to the adjacency interconnect register
2	CORW NUM	IO← Inter R	The processor reads the adjacency interconnection register data to the adjacency interconnection interface
3	CORRL RD,RL	RD←RL	The processor reads the adjacent data into the general register file
4	CORRS RL,RS	RL←RS	The processor writes data from the general register file to the adjacency interconnect register

In addition, this processor also realizes the basic instruction set of RV32I, ALU also has a two-level pipelining multiplier, can realize multiplication operation [9].

This image has been removed due to copyright issues.

Figure 2.2 : Adjacency interconnection mechanism simulation waveform [9]

The suggested processor is prototyped on the FPGA development board BASYS 3 and implemented in Verilog HDL. The CPU runs at 100 MHz, and the Slice Registers and Slice LUTS take up 3816 and 2131, respectively, of RAM [9].

2.5 Design and Implementation of a RISC V Processor on FPGA

The design, implementation into a Field Programmable Gate Array (FPGA), and testing of a low-power, open-source RISC-V processor employing contemporary hardware design methodologies. Their goal was to develop a RISC-V processor that would be simple enough for newcomers to understand and light enough to be used on even tiny FPGAs [10].

In modern processors, they have reduced the usage of components and conventions that are not strictly required for a barebones implementation. For instance, the CPU has a straightforward Harvard architecture and no pipelining [10].

Table 2.5 : FPGA Utilization Metrics [10]

Resource	Utilization	Utilization%
Look-up tables	322	1.55
Flip – Flops	229	0.55
IO	18	16.98

System Verilog is used to write the implementation of each component and the associated test benches in a clear and normal way. A RISC-V processor with files intended for the Basys 3 Artix-7 FPGA was the result of the project. With extremely low resource consumption on the FPGA, performance was evaluated using the Dhyrstone benchmark and reached a robust 2276 DMIPs/MHz, even surpassing the ARM Cortex-A9 [10].

This image has been removed due to copyright issues.

Figure 2.3 : Dhyrstone Benchmark Performance [10]

2.6 Implementation of the RISC-V Architecture with the Extended Zbb Instruction Set

Automation and process control systems in electrical power engineering are only two of the many applications that can benefit from the standard modifications to the basic instruction set architecture defined by the RISC-V architectural specification. One of the helpful additions is the bit manipulation extension, whose algorithms were first developed by ARM and Intel to reduce power consumption and increase performance [11].

A Verilog language implementation of the Zbb extension for simple bit manipulation. The designed module is incorporated into the soft processor core of the schoolRISCV. The ModelSim program was used to model it and verify that it was operating correctly. Terasic DEI-SoC FPGA board was used for prototype and synthesis of the CPU [11].

Table 2.6 : Comparison of Processor Cores with Basic and Extended Architecture [11]

Characteristic	Core with basic architecture	Core with extended architecture
Maximum clock frequency, Fmax	104.35 MHz	54.82 MHz
Amount of FPGA logic cells	99	986
Amount of resisters	103	821
Amount of memory cells	768	768
Amount of pins	141	141

The expanded core's performance studies revealed an average acceleration of 29.9% in program execution and a 37.5% decrease in memory occupied. A higher number of logic components and registers were used in order to accomplish the performance gain [11].

2.7 A RISC-V ISA Compatible Processor IP

A high-performance general-purpose processor system based on the open-source RISC-V instruction set architecture is developed [12].The CPU supports virtual memory and features a 32-bit, 5-stage pipeline core with independent8 KB I-cache and D-cache. The processor is capable of processing the RISC-V ISA's integer, atomic, and floating-point (single and double precision) instruction subset. To enhance the system's real-time performance, a specialized floating-point execution unit and a nested vectored interrupt unit are incorporated [12].

Table 2.7 : Prediction accuracy improvement [12]

Benchmarks	Without BPU	With BPU
Dhrystone	33.94%	97.78%
CoreMark	40.02%	89.62%

Table 2.8 : Performance improvement in synthetic benchmarks [12]

Benchmark	Without BPU	With BPU
Dhrystone	0.7132 DMIPS/MHz	0.9812 DMIPS/MHz
CoreMark	2.66/MHz	3.32/MHz

A branch prediction unit and a hardware Economic Value Added replacement policy for I-Cache and D-Cache are implemented to increase the processor's execution speed. The processor's CoreMark number, which is 3.32 CoreMark/MHz, is used to assess its performance. The maximum clock frequency of the design, which is implemented on Xilinx's Virtex-7 (XC7VX485tffg1761-2) FPGA, is 60MHz [12].

2.8 Implementation and Extension of Bit Manipulation Instruction on RISC-V Architecture using FPGA

ARM and Intel introduced Bit Manipulation Instructions (BMIs) to increase the program's power dissipation and runtime efficiency, even though RISC-V ISA is widely used and currently only supports two basic BMIs [13].Concentrates on developing low-cost embedded/Internet of things systems by optimizing power, cost, and design complexity. It presents a simplified architecture of a fully synthesizable 32-bit processor, known as "bitRISC," based on the open-source RISC-V (RV32I) ISA and introduces two new RISC-V BMIs, which are implemented on our designed processor [13].

Table 2.9 : Resource Utilization [13]

Resources	Utilization	Available	Utilization%
LUT	2312	53200	4.35
LUTRAM	62	17400	0.36
FF	2035	106400	1.91
IO	21	200	10.50
BUFG	13	32	40.63

Using Verilog HDL and a compressed architecture, the "bitRISC" is a single-cycle processor that is further prototyped on the FPGA "ZedBoard." A design can achieve an operating clock frequency of up to 100MHz. According to reports, the chip uses 1.109W of power total [13].

2.9 Comprehensive Analysis

Table 2.10 Comprehensive Analysis

Research Paper	Architecture	Instruction Set	Operating Frequency/Clock Speed	Power	Work done	Comments
[6]	RISC-V micro-architecture	RV32	32 MHz	7.9mW	Pipeline effect on functionality	To increase processor performance

[7]	Austere RISC-V	RV32I	105 MHz & 111.5 MHz	-	Cryptographic protection mechanism	To provide security mechanism
[8]	64-bit RISC-V architecture	RV64I	140.398 MHz	0.037W	Low cost embedded device	To reduce the overall cost
[9]	RISC-V architecture	RV32I	100 MHz	-	Adjacent interconnected reconfigurable array by adding some special instruction	To increase performance
[10]	RISC-V architecture	RV64I reduced version	100 MHz	-	Modern hardware design techniques for beginners	To make light weight processor
[11]	SchoolRISC-V soft core processor	RV32I-Zbb	54.82 MHz	-	Zbb extension bit manipulation	To increase performance
[12]	32-bit 5 stage	-	60 MHz	-	Pipeline architecture	To improve performance

					with 8KB Icache and Dcache	real time speed
	pipeline			–		
[13]	RISC-V ISA	RV32I	100 MHz	1.109 W	Low cost embedded device	To optimize the power and cost
[14]	biRISC-V	-	-	-	Superscalar dual issue design	To increase the throughput.

According to this analysis, there are various variants of RISC-V, and these variants are used for various purposes, such as lowering overall costs, enhancing overall performance, speeding up processor execution, lowering power consumption, creating a more manageable and compact version of the original architecture to take up less space, etc.The superscalar dual issue design of the biRISC-V processor increases the unit's overall throughput. The CPU can issue some pairs of instructions at once in order to increase instruction throughput. Therefore, the main goal of this study is to try to comprehend how this biRISC-V processor functions and to try to implement the fetch unit, decode unit, execute unit, ALU unit, issue unit, and program counter unit by creating a testbench and seeing the results of the performance simulation.

Chapter 3 Conclusion

Because of its modular, scalable, and adaptable architecture, RISC-V can be used in a variety of applications. Its adaptability, simplicity, and efficiency are contributing to its increasing popularity. There are various RISC-V versions, and each variant serves a different function. For example, it can be used to lower overall costs, boost processor performance, lower power consumption, or create a more compact version of the original design.the most recent and promising member of the RISC-V family is the 32-bit biRISC-V processor core, according to our review of the literature. Superscalar dual issue design is used by the 32-bit biRISC-V processor core to increase processor throughput overall.

REFERENCES

[1] A. Waterman, Y. Lee, D. A. Patterson, and K. Asanovic, "The RISC-V instruction set manual, volume I: User-level ISA," Dept. EECS, Univ. California, Berkeley, Berkeley, CA, USA, Tech. Rep. 22, May 2017. [Online]. Available: https://riscv.org/wp- content/uploads/2017/05/riscvspec-v2.2.pdf

[2] Andrew Waterman, Yunsup Lee, David Patterson, Krste Asanović, "The RISC-V Instruction Set Manual,   Volume   I: User-Level   ISA   Version   2.1", Technical Report UCB/EECS-2016-118, EECS Department, University of California, Berkeley, May   31,   2016.   Specifications   –   RISC-V   International.   (n.d.). https://riscv.org/technical/specifications/

[3] A. Waterman, Y. Lee, D. Patterson, K. Asanović, Electrical Engineering and Computer Sciences, and University of California at Berkeley, "The RISC-V Instruction Set Manual, Volume I: User-Level   ISA,   Version   2.1,"   May   2016.   [Online].   Available: https://www2.eecs.berkeley.edu/Pubs/TechRpts/2016/EECS-2016-118.pdf

[4] Waterman, A., Lee, Y., Patterson, D., Asanovic, K., Electrical Engineering and Computer Sciences, & University of California at Berkeley. (2014). The RISC-V Instruction Set Manual, Volume I: User-Level ISA, Version 2.0. In Technical Report No. UCB/EECS-2014-54. https://www2.eecs.berkeley.edu/Pubs/TechRpts/2014/EECS-2014-54.pdf

[5] A. Waterman, Y. Lee, D. Patterson, K. Asanovic, Electrical Engineering and Computer Sciences, and University of California at Berkeley, "The RISC-V Instruction Set Manual, Volume I: Base User-Level ISA," May 2011. [Online]. Available: https://www2.eecs.berkeley.edu/Pubs/TechRpts/2011/EECS-2011-62.pdf

[6] D. K. Dennis et al., "Single cycle RISC-V micro architecture processor and its FPGA prototype," 2017 7th International Symposium on Embedded Computing and System Design (ISED), Durgapur, India, 2017, pp. 1-5, doi: 10.1109/ISED.2017.8303926.

[7] Z. Zang, Y. Liu and R. C. C. Cheung, "Reconfigurable RISC-V Secure Processor And SoC Integration," 2019 IEEE International Conference on Industrial Technology (ICIT), Melbourne, VIC, Australia, 2019, pp. 827-832, doi: 10.1109/ICIT.2019.8755206.

[8] "SINGLE CYCLE 64-BIT RISC-V PROCESSOR AND IT'S FPGA PROTOTYPE", International Journal of Emerging Technologies and Innovative Research (www.jetir.org | UGC and issn Approved), ISSN:2349-5162, Vol.5, Issue 8, page no. pp644-650, August-2018, Available at : http://www.jetir.org/papers/JETIR1807555.pdf

[9] Y. Lu, Y. Liu, Y. Liao, Y. Liu and L. Xu, "Design of Adjacent Interconnect Processor Based on RISC-V," 2021 IEEE 4th International Conference on Electronics Technology (ICET), Chengdu, China, 2021, pp. 427-431, doi: 10.1109/ICET51757.2021.9451102.

[10] L. Poli, S. Saha, X. Zhai and K. D. Mcdonald-Maier, "Design and Implementation of a RISC V Processor on FPGA," 2021 17th International Conference on Mobility, Sensing and Networking (MSN), Exeter, United Kingdom, 2021, pp. 161-166, doi: 10.1109/MSN53354.2021.00037.

[11] Markov and A. Romanov, "Implementation of the RISC-V Architecture with the Extended Zbb Instruction Set," 2022 International Ural Conference on Electrical Power Engineering (UralCon), Magnitogorsk, Russian Federation, 2022, pp. 180-184, doi: 10.1109/UralCon54942.2022.9906776.

[12] S. Budi, P. Gupta, K. Varghese and A. Bharadwaj, "A RISC-V ISA compatible processor IP for SoC," 2018 International Symposium on Devices, Circuits and Systems (ISDCS), Howrah, India, 2018, pp. 1-5, doi: 10.1109/ISDCS.2018.8379629.

[13] V. Jain, A. Sharma and E. A. Bezerra, "Implementation and Extension of Bit Manipulation Instruction on RISC-V Architecture using FPGA," 2020 IEEE 9th International Conference on Communication Systems and Network Technologies (CSNT), Gwalior, India, 2020, pp. 167-172, doi: 10.1109/CSNT48778.2020.9115759.

[14] Kuopinghsu. (n.d.). GitHub - kuopinghsu/biriscv: biRISC-V - 32-bit dual issue RISC-V CPU Software Environment. GitHub. https://github.com/kuopinghsu/biriscv/tree/main

[15] Dongarra, J., Łuszczek, P., Wolf, F., Träff, J. L., Quinton, P., Hellwagner, H., Fränzle, M., Lengauer, C., Ceze, L., Hiraki, K., Riesen, R., Maccabe, A. B., Feo, J., Madduri, K., Risset, T., Khan, M., Kumar, V., Marathe, M. V., Stretz, P. E., . . . Reinders, J. (2011). Superscalar Processors. In Springer eBooks (pp. 1962–1966). https://doi.org/10.1007/978-0-387-09766- 4_280